EXPERT CONSULTATION AND MENTORING

SMOOTH SAILING THROUGH

GOVERNMENT PROJECTS

EXPERT CONSULTATION AND MENTORING

SMOOTH SAILING THROUGH

GOVERNMENT PROJECTS

DR. SIYA SETH

Worldwide Published by
Pendown Press

PENDOWN PRESS LLP
An ISO 9001 & ISO 14001 Certified Co.,
Regd. Office: 3767A, Kanhaiya Nagar,
Tri Nagar, Delhi-110035
Ph.: 8130886000, 9650072927, 8595249536
E-mail: info@pendownpress.com
Branch Office: 1A/2A, 20, Hari Sadan, Ansari Road,
Daryaganj, New Delhi-110002
Ph.: 011-45794768
Website: PendownPress.com

First Edition: 2023
Price: ₹999/-
ISBN: 978-93-5554-678-4

Layout and Cover Designed by Pendown Graphics Team
Printed and Bound in India by Thomson Press India Ltd.

Contents

- Understanding the structure and hierarchy of government organizations
- Roles and responsibilities of different government departments
- Interdepartmental coordination and collaboration
- Building effective relationships with colleagues and superiors

- Understanding the bidding process and its various stages
- Preparing and submitting responsive bids
- Compliance with bidding requirements and documentation
- Evaluating bid opportunities and assessing risks
- Strategies for competitive pricing and cost management

- Defining your project acquisition goals and objectives
- Conducting market research and identifying opportunities
- Developing a comprehensive project acquisition strategy
- Creating a compelling value proposition for government agencies
- Understanding the proposal and bidding process

About Author

Dr. Siya Seth is a dynamic and accomplished entrepreneur with 26 years of extensive experience in the government sector. With a successful track record of executing over 150 government projects and acquiring 270 projects, she is renowned for her expertise in social development, corporate networking, and government initiatives in both India and Africa.

Dr. Siya Seth's visionary leadership and innovative approach have propelled her ventures to great heights of success. Her companies, including Spherion Solutions Pvt. Ltd. and Sumdrishti Education Society, have become synonymous with excellence and innovation in their respective industries.

As an executive board member of Vaishya Cooperative Bank, Dr. Siya Seth brings her financial acumen and strategic decision-making skills to drive the bank's growth and success. Her ability to navigate complex business landscapes, adhere to ethical standards, and deliver impactful outcomes has earned her the respect of colleagues and stakeholders alike.

Dr. Siya Seth's commitment to creating a positive impact extends beyond her professional endeavors. She actively contributes to society through her involvement in social development and education initiatives.

In her book, "Smooth Sailing Through Government Project," Dr. Siya Seth generously shares her wealth of experience and expertise. Through insightful chapters on project acquisition, strategic partnerships, effective project management, and policy implementation, she provides valuable guidance to navigate the intricacies of government work. With a crisp and interactive writing style, Dr. Siya Seth engages readers and equips them with the knowledge and skills needed to thrive in the government sector.

Foreword

It is my distinct pleasure to write the foreword for the book "Smooth Sailing Through Government Project," authored by a team of experienced professionals who have dedicated themselves to simplifying the intricacies of working within the government sector.

Having personally worked on and completed government projects for over two decades, I am acutely aware of the challenges and nuances that individuals and organizations encounter when engaging in government work. The complex nature of the public sector, with its regulations, procedures, and unique dynamics, can often appear daunting to those seeking to navigate through it successfully.

In "Smooth Sailing Through Government Project," the authors have not only captured the essence of the government work landscape but also provided practical insights and guidance that will empower readers to excel in this field. Drawing upon their extensive experience, the authors have compiled a comprehensive guide that demystifies the government procurement process, equips readers with essential knowledge, and imparts valuable skills necessary for success.

One of the book's greatest strengths lies in its practical approach. The authors have gone beyond theory and provided readers with interactive exercises, case studies, and simulations that facilitate a hands-on learning experience. By engaging readers in this manner, the authors have ensured that the knowledge gained from the book can be immediately applied in real-world scenarios, enhancing the effectiveness and relevance of the content.

I commend the authors for their dedication to sharing their collective wisdom and experiences in this book. Their commitment to making government work accessible and manageable is evident throughout the pages, making "Smooth Sailing Through Government Project" an indispensable guide for anyone involved in government projects.

Dr. Siya Seth

Serial Entrepreneur

Acknowledgement

Writing a book is a collaborative effort that involves the support, contributions, and encouragement of many individuals. I would like to express my deep heartfelt gratitude to all those who have played a significant role in the creation and publication of this book.

First and foremost, I would like to thank my family and friends for their unwavering support throughout this journey. Your belief in me and constant encouragement have been invaluable. Your patience, understanding, and words of encouragement have fueled my motivation and kept me focused during the writing process.

I extend my heartfelt appreciation to my editor and the publishing team for their dedication, guidance, and expertise in shaping this book. Your insightful feedback, meticulous editing, and unwavering commitment to excellence have been instrumental in bringing this project to fruition.

I am deeply grateful to the readers who have shown interest in this book. Your enthusiasm and support inspire me to continue sharing my experiences and knowledge. I hope that the insights and lessons offered in this book resonate with you and contribute to your personal growth and development.

Lastly, I want to express my sincere gratitude to all the individuals who work tirelessly in the publishing industry, including agents, designers, marketers, and booksellers. Your commitment to bringing books to readers is truly commendable, and I am grateful for your invaluable contributions to the literary world.

To everyone who has been a part of this journey, whether directly or indirectly, your contributions have been invaluable. Thank you for being a part of this book and for turning it into a reality.

Chapter 1

Navigating The Government System

Introduction

Understand the critical nature of navigating the government system for professionals working within government organizations. Gain an overview of the structure and hierarchy of government organizations. Explore the roles and responsibilities of different government departments. Understand interdepartmental coordination and collaboration, as well as building effective relationships with colleagues and superiors.

Section 1

Understanding the Structure and Hierarchy of Government Organizations

- Explore the hierarchical structure commonly found in government organizations.

- Gain insights into the roles of central government agencies, ministries, departments, and local government bodies.

- Engage with an interactive visual representation of the structure of a government organization.

Section 2

Roles and Responsibilities of Different Government Departments

- Dive into the specific functions of key government departments, such as finance, health, education, transportation, and defense.

- Connect government departments with their respective roles and responsibilities.

- Develop a comprehensive understanding of the diverse functions within the government system.

Section 3

Interdepartmental Coordination and Collaboration

- Gain an understanding of the criticality of interdepartmental coordination for efficient service delivery.

- Identify and address challenges that may arise during collaborative efforts.

- Explore effective strategies to foster collaboration, including cross-departmental task forces and resource sharing.

- Engage in an interactive simulation to experience the complexities of interdepartmental coordination.

Section 4

Building Effective Relationships with Colleagues and Superiors

- Discover effective strategies for fostering positive working relationships.

- Enhance communication skills, active listening, empathy, and teamwork.

- Understand the importance of organizational dynamics, hierarchies, and protocols.

- Practice effective communication and relationship-building through interactive role-playing exercises within a government context.

Chapter 2

Navigating The Bidding Process

Introduction

The bidding process plays a crucial role in obtaining government projects. For vendors seeking to secure government contracts, it is essential to navigating the bidding process effectively. Gain a comprehensive understanding of the bidding process, including its various stages, strategies for preparing and submitting responsive bids, compliance with bidding requirements and documentation, evaluation of bid opportunities, and risks assessment. Furthermore, explore techniques for competitive pricing and effective cost management to increase the chances of success in government bids.

Understanding the Bidding Process and Its Various Stages

The bidding process involves several stages, each requiring careful attention and preparation. This section outlines the key stages, from the initial announcement of the procurement opportunity to contract award. We cover stages such as pre-qualification, request for information (RFI), request for proposal (RFP), bid evaluation, and contract negotiation. Acquiring a clear understanding of the sequence and significance of these stages is imperative for vendors to effectively participate in government bids.

Preparing and Submitting Responsive Bids

Preparing and submitting a responsive bid is crucial for success in government procurement. Vendors must thoroughly review bid documents, including the RFP, to understand the scope of work, technical requirements, evaluation criteria, and submission guidelines. This section provides guidance on the bid preparation process, emphasizing the importance of addressing all mandatory requirements, offering innovative solutions, and showcasing the organization's unique strengths and qualifications. Additionally, timely and accurate bid submission is also highlighted to ensure compliance with deadlines and avoid disqualification.

Compliance with Bidding Requirements and Documentation

Compliance with bidding requirements is fundamental. Government agencies establish precise guidelines and criteria to ensure a fair and transparent procurement process. Vendors must strictly adhere to these requirements and provide all necessary documentation to validate their eligibility and capability to undertake the project. This section emphasizes the significance of meeting compliance standards, addressing any pre-qualification criteria, and furnishing accurate and complete documentation to gain a competitive edge.

Evaluating Bid Opportunities and Assessing Risks

Evaluating bid opportunities is essential for vendors to allocate their resources and efforts effectively towards viable prospects. This section explores the criteria for evaluating bid opportunities, including project alignment with the organization's capabilities, financial viability, risk assessment, and strategic fit. By conducting a thorough risk analysis, vendors can identify potential challenges and develop mitigation strategies to enhance their chances of success in the bidding process.

Strategies for Competitive Pricing and Cost Management

Competitive pricing is a crucial factor in securing government contracts. This section explores various pricing strategies, including cost-based pricing, value-based pricing, and competitive pricing analysis. Vendors must find a balance between offering competitive prices while ensuring profitability and delivering quality. Additionally, effective cost management techniques such as cost estimation, cost control, and cost optimization, are discussed to enhance cost-effectiveness and project viability.

By mastering the intricacies of the bidding process, vendors can position themselves as strong contenders in government projects, unlocking new opportunities for growth and success.

Chapter 3

Preparing For Project Acquisition

Introduction

Preparing for project acquisition in the government sector demands careful planning, research, and strategic thinking. This section focuses on essential steps to ensure a successful approach to securing government projects. By defining clear goals and objectives, conducting thorough market research, developing a comprehensive project acquisition strategy, creating a compelling value proposition, and understanding the proposal and bidding process, organizations can position themselves for success in acquiring government projects.

Defining Your Project Acquisition Goals and Objectives

- Gain a clear understanding your organization's strengths, capabilities, and strategic direction.

- Identify the types of projects that align with your expertise and resources.

- Set specific, measurable, achievable, relevant, and time-bound (SMART) objectives to guide your efforts effectively.

Conducting Market Research and Identifying Opportunities

- Identify specific government sectors or industries that require your products or services.

- Analyze past government projects to gain valuable insights into potential opportunities and involved agencies.

- Study government initiatives, budgets, and future plans to identify upcoming projects.

- Gather valuable market intelligence from industry experts, associations, and government stakeholders to stay informed about trends and opportunities.

Developing a Comprehensive Project Acquisition Strategy

- Align your strategy with overall business objectives and budget constraints.

- Consider risk assessment, resource allocation, and target regions.

- Create a well-defined timeline with clear milestones to track progress and make necessary strategy adjustments.

- Incorporate flexibility to adapt to changing market conditions and emerging opportunities.

Creating a Compelling Value Proposition for Government Agencies

- Tailor your value proposition to address the specific needs of government agencies.

- Demonstrate how your products or services can offer cost savings, improved efficiency, or better outcomes.

- Highlight your organization's track record, experience, and success stories to build credibility and trust.

- Understanding the Proposal and Bidding Process.

Review RFPs carefully to grasp the agency's requirements, evaluation criteria, and submission guidelines

- Seek clarification on any ambiguities and strictly adhere to deadlines.

- Prepare a responsive and competitive proposal that showcases your unique strengths and qualifications.

By following these steps, organizations can navigate the complexities of government project acquisition effectively, increasing their chances of success and contributing to meaningful projects that benefit society.

Chapter 4

Crafting Winning Proposals

Introduction

Crafting a winning proposal is an essential skill for organizations seeking to secure government projects. A well-crafted proposal not only demonstrates your capabilities and qualifications but also addresses the specific needs and requirements of the government agency. In this chapter, we delve into the essential elements of a successful government proposal. This includes tailoring the proposal, creating a concise executive summary, showcasing capabilities, and emphasizing your competitive advantage and value proposition.

Understanding the Elements of a Successful Government Proposal

A successful government proposal is a comprehensive and compelling document that effectively communicates your organization's ability to deliver the desired outcomes. It typically includes several key elements:

▶ **Cover Page:**

A professional cover page containing the project title, your organization's name, logo, and contact information.

▶ **Table of Contents:**

A detailed table of contents that facilitates easy navigation for evaluators.

▶ **Executive Summary:**

A concise overview of the proposal's key points, highlighting the most critical aspects of your offering.

▶ **Project Introduction:**

A brief introduction to your organization, highlighting your mission, values, and track record.

▶ **Understanding of Requirements:**

A clear and comprehensive understanding of the government agency's needs and how your proposal addresses them.

▶ **Technical Approach:**

Present a detailed description of your approach to overcome the agency's challenges and accomplish project's objectives.

▶ **Methodology:**

A step-by-step explanation of how you plan to execute the project, including timelines, milestones, and deliverables.

▶ **Qualifications and Experience:**

Showcase your organization's relevant qualifications, experience, and expertise in similar projects as evidence of your capability to successfully undertake the proposed project.

▶ **Personnel and Team Structure:**

Introduce the key personnel who will be involved in the project, highlighting their qualifications and respective roles.

▶ **Budget and Pricing:**

Provide a transparent and well-structured budget that outlines all costs associated with the project.

▶ **Risk Assessment and Mitigation:**

Conduct a comprehensive analysis of potential risks and present an effective plan to mitigate them.

▶ **References and Testimonials:**

Include statements from satisfied clients and partners that validate your organization's capabilities.

Tailoring Your Proposal to Meet Government Agency Requirements:

When creating a proposal for a government agency, it's important to customize it to their specific needs. Here are some key points to consider:

▶ **Research:**

Thoroughly study the agency to understand their goals, challenges, and priorities.

▶ **Address Objectives:**

Show how your solution aligns with the agency's objectives and solves their problems.

▶ **Follow Guidelines:**

Stick to the agency's formatting and submission requirements.

▶ **Use Appropriate Language:**

Adapt your language and tone to match the agency's culture and industry.

▶ **Showcase Experience:**

Highlight relevant past projects to demonstrate your expertise.

▶ **Provide Supporting Documents:**

Include case studies, certifications, or testimonials to back up your claims.

▶ **Demonstrate Compliance:**

Explain how your proposal meets all legal and regulatory requirements.

By tailoring your proposal to meet the agency's requirements, you increase your chances of success and show your commitment to understanding their needs.

Chapter 5

Research And Data Analysis

Introduction

In government work, research and data analysis are essential for policy development and decision-making. This chapter delves into the significance of research and data analysis, methods for conducting research, techniques for data gathering, principles of data analysis, and the utilization of data for evidence-based decision-making.

The Importance of Research and Data Analysis in Government

Research and data analysis plays a crucial role in effective governance and policy making. They provide valuable insights into complex issues, facilitate evidence-based decision-making, and support the development and evaluation of policies. By conducting thorough research and data analysis, governments can gain a deeper understanding of societal needs, assess the impacts of policies, identify trends, and allocate resources efficiently.

Methods for Conducting Research

To ensure high-quality research, government officials need to adopt a systematic approach. This section covers various research methods, including qualitative and quantitative research, case studies, literature reviews, surveys, interviews, and focus groups. The strengths and limitations of each method are discussed, aiding officials in selecting the appropriate approach based on research objectives and available resources.

Techniques for Gathering Reliable and Relevant Data

Gathering reliable and relevant data is vital for drawing accurate conclusions and making informed decisions. This section of the chapter focuses on techniques for data collection, including primary data collection through surveys and interviews, as well as secondary data collection through existing records, databases, and public sources. It emphasizes the importance of data quality, validity, reliability, and ethical considerations in the data collection process.

Principles of Data Analysis

Data analysis involves transforming raw data into meaningful insights. This section covers the principles of data analysis, including data cleaning, transformation, visualization, and statistical analysis. It explores software tools for data analysis, such as spreadsheets and statistical packages. Additionally, it emphasizes the importance of using appropriate analysis methods, addressing biases, and considering limitations in the interpretation process.

Analyzing and Interpreting Data

Once data is collected and analyzed, interpreting the findings becomes crucial. This section provides guidance for government officials on how to interpret data within the context of research objectives and policy goals. It discusses techniques for identifying patterns, trends, and correlations in the data. Furthermore, it emphasizes the significance of considering biases and limitations during the interpretation process.

Presenting Research Findings in a Clear and Concise Manner

Effectively communicating research findings is vital to inform decision-makers and the public. This section explores various methods of presenting research findings clearly and concisely, such as reports, data visualizations, infographics, and presentations. It emphasizes the importance of tailoring the communication style to the target audience and utilizing visuals to make complex information more accessible.

Utilizing Data to Drive Evidence-Based Decision-Making

Evidence-based decision-making is crucial for effective governance. This section of the chapter explores how research findings and data analysis inform policy development and decision-making. It highlights how evidence-based decision-making enhances the quality of policies, improves resource allocation, and fosters public trust in government actions. Additionally, it presents examples of successful evidence-based policymaking in various government sectors.

By understanding the principles of research and data analysis, government officials can make more informed decisions, develop effective policies, and address societal challenges with an evidence-based approach.

Chapter 6

Mastering Time And Task Management

Introduction

Proficient time and task management are crucial skills for professionals working in the government sector. This chapter explores the significance of prioritization in government work, setting clear goals and objectives, effective time management techniques, delegating tasks and managing deadlines, and strategies to handle numerous projects simultaneously. By mastering these skills, individuals can enhance their productivity, meet deadlines, and successfully manage their workload in the government environment.

Section 1

Importance of Prioritization in Government Work

Prioritization is a fundamental aspect of managing government work efficiently and effectively. In this section, we will emphasize the importance of prioritizing tasks based on their urgency, importance, and alignment with organizational goals. We will examine the potential consequences that arise from poor prioritization and provide practical tips for assessing and categorizing tasks to determine their priority level. An interactive exercise will allow readers to practice prioritizing tasks in a simulated government work scenario, enabling them to grasp the impact of effective prioritization on productivity and desired outcomes.

Section 2

Setting Clear Goals and Objectives

In government work, having well-defined goals and objectives is essential for establishing a sense of direction and purpose in government work. This section will delve into the process of setting SMART (Specific, Measurable, Achievable, Relevant, Time-bound) goals and objectives, aligning them with organizational priorities, and communicating them effectively. We will explore strategies for breaking down goals into manageable tasks and developing action plans to achieve them. An interactive goal-setting exercise will guide readers through the process of setting goals and creating action plans for a government-related project.

Section 3

Effective Time Management Techniques

Effective time management is essential for optimizing productivity and meeting deadlines. In this section, we will introduce various time management techniques, such as creating to-do lists, using calendars and scheduling tools, implementing the Pomodoro Technique, and minimizing distractions. Furthermore, we will provide practical tips for managing interruptions and maintaining focus on high-priority tasks. An interactive time management tool will allow readers to plan and organize their tasks, set reminders, and track their progress, enhancing their time management skills.

Section 4

Delegating Tasks and Managing Deadlines

Delegating tasks and managing deadlines are crucial skills for government professionals. This section will delve into the significance of delegation, highlighting its benefits such as workload distribution, skill development, and fostering teamwork. We will explore strategies for effective delegation, such as assessing task suitability, communicating expectations clearly, providing essential resources and support, and monitoring progress. Additionally, we will address techniques for managing deadlines, including setting realistic deadlines, identifying critical path tasks, and leveraging project management tools. An interactive case study will be there to challenge readers to delegate tasks and manage deadlines in a government project scenario, allowing them to practice their delegation and deadline management skills.

Section 5

Strategies for Handling Multiple Projects Simultaneously

Government professionals often juggle multiple projects concurrently. This section will provide strategies for effectively handling multiple projects, such as prioritizing projects, managing resources, establishing clear communication channels, and practicing efficient task switching. We will discuss techniques for managing project dependencies, monitoring progress, and mitigating risks. An interactive project management simulation will immerse readers in a scenario where they must manage multiple projects simultaneously, enabling them to apply their skills and make informed decisions in a multi-project environment.

Chapter 7

Budgeting And Financial Management

Introduction

Budgeting and financial management are integral to the proper allocation of resources in government projects. This chapter offers an in-depth overview of the government budgeting process, financial management principles, effective resource allocation, expenditure control and tracking. It emphasizes the importance of ensuring accountability and transparency in financial management. Each section is presented with interactive elements and tables to engage readers and provide practical insights into the topic.

Section 1

Overview of Government Budgeting Process

In this section, we introduce an interactive flowchart that outlines step-by-step overview of the government budgeting process. Readers can navigate through each stage, from budget formulation to execution and monitoring. The flowchart will prominently feature key decision points, the participation of different stakeholders, and the role of legislative bodies in the budget approval process. Additionally, concise explanations of each stage will be provided to offer a comprehensive understanding of the budgeting process.

Section 2

Understanding Financial Management Principles

Effective financial management is crucial to ensure the efficient use of public funds. This section will feature interactive elements, such as pop-up definitions and tooltips, to explain essential financial management principles. We will cover topics like fiscal responsibility, cost-effectiveness, long-term planning, and risk management. By using interactive elements, readers can gain a clear grasp of the principles and their practical application in government project financing.

Section 3

Allocating Resources Effectively

Effective resource allocation is fundamental to achieving project goals and objectives. In this section, we will present a table that outlines different methods of resource allocation, such as incremental budgeting, performance-based budgeting, and zero-based budgeting. The table will compare the strengths and weaknesses of each method, and interactive cells will provide real-world examples of government projects that have successfully utilized specific resource allocation approaches.

Section 4

Controlling and Tracking Expenditures

Controlling and tracking expenditures play a vital role in ensuring financial discipline and avoiding budget overruns. To illustrate best practices, we will present an interactive checklist for financial managers to track project expenditures. This checklist will encompass expense categorization, approval processes, expense monitoring, and periodic reporting. Interactive features will allow readers to click on each item to access detailed explanations and downloadable templates for facilitating practical implementation of these best practices.

Section 5

Ensuring Accountability and Transparency in Financial Management

Accountability and transparency are essential for fostering public trust and confidence in government financial management. In this section, we will present a case study with interactive elements, showcasing a successful government project that prioritized accountability and transparency. Readers can click on interactive markers to access relevant project documents, financial reports, and statements from stakeholders. These resources will demonstrate how transparency measures enhanced the project outcomes.

Chapter 8

Building Strategic Partnerships And Alliances

Introduction

In the realm of government project acquisition, cultivating strategic partnerships and alliances is a potent strategy for achieving success. Collaboration with other vendors, subcontractors, suppliers, and various stakeholders can enhance an organization's capabilities, resources, and competitive advantage. This chapter explores the importance of leveraging partnerships, methods for identifying potential partners and collaborators, strategies for establishing mutually beneficial relationships, the creation of strategic alliances, and the benefits of collaborating with subcontractors and suppliers.

Leveraging Partnerships for Government Project Acquisition

Partnerships and alliances play a pivotal role in government project acquisition. Collaborating with other organizations can grant access to complementary expertise, resources, and geographic reach. Through strategic partnerships, vendors can strengthen their capacity to respond to complex government projects that demand a diverse set of skills and capabilities. Additionally, partnering with established organizations can increase the credibility and trustworthiness of vendors, which are critical factors in winning government contracts.

Identifying Potential Partners and Collaborators

The first step in building strategic partnerships is identifying potential partners and collaborators. Organizations should conduct thorough market research to identify other vendors, subcontractors, or suppliers that complement their strengths and align with their business objectives. It is advisable to seek out organizations with a track record of successful government project acquisition and a reputation for delivering high-quality work. Active engagement in industry events, networking, and attending procurement-related forums can help identify suitable partners.

Establishing Mutually Beneficial Relationships with Other Vendors

Building successful partnerships requires a focus on mutual benefit. Organizations should approach potential partners with a clear understanding of what each party can bring to the table. Clearly articulate the value proposition and benefits of collaborating, highlighting how the partnership will enhance capabilities, increase efficiency, or open up new market opportunities. Be open to negotiation and find ways to ensure that both parties gain value from the relationship.

Creating Strategic Alliances to Enhance Competitive Advantage

Strategic alliances are formed when organizations with complementary capabilities and resources come together to pursue specific opportunities jointly. This section explores the process of creating strategic alliances and the array of benefits they offer. When forming strategic alliances, vendors must establish clear objectives, delineate responsibilities, and define governance structures. By doing so, an effective alliance can provide a competitive advantage, as organizations can pool their expertise, share risks and resources, and present a unified and stronger proposal to government agencies.

Collaborating with Subcontractors and Suppliers

Collaborating with subcontractors and suppliers is another essential aspect of building strategic partnerships. Subcontractors can contribute specialized skills or resources to the project, enabling the primary vendor to offer a more comprehensive solution. Meanwhile, suppliers play a crucial role in providing the necessary materials or equipment for project execution. This section explores best practices for selecting reliable subcontractors and suppliers, negotiating favorable agreements, and managing relationships effectively.

The Benefits of Collaborative Approach

Collaborative approaches offer numerous benefits for government project acquisition. By working with partners, organizations can enhance their capabilities, expand their geographic reach, and gain access to new markets. Collaborative efforts can also result in improved innovation through the exchange of knowledge and ideas. Additionally, forming strategic alliances or collaborating with subcontractors and suppliers can reduce project risks, increase operational efficiency, and contribute to cost savings.

Chapter 9

Effective Project Management in the Government Sector

Introduction

Project management plays a vital role in the successful execution of government projects. This chapter explores the key aspects of effective project management in the government sector, including understanding government project management frameworks, planning and executing projects, managing project scope, time, and resources, adhering to government reporting and documentation requirements, and mitigating risks to ensure project success. The content of this chapter will be presented in an interactive and interesting manner to engage readers and provide practical insights into government project management.

Section 1

Understanding Government Project Management Frameworks

In this section, we will acquaint readers with various government project management frameworks and methodologies, such as PRINCE2 (Projects in Controlled Environments) and PMBOK (Project Management Body of Knowledge). To engage readers, an interactive quiz will be incorporated, allowing them to assess their knowledge and understanding of these frameworks.. Additionally, we will provide real-life examples of government projects that have successfully implemented these frameworks, highlighting their benefits and key principles.

Section 2

Planning and Executing Government Projects Effectively

Effective project planning and execution are crucial for achieving project objectives. In this section, we will introduce an interactive case study of a government project, where readers can actively make decisions at different stages of the project. Each decision made will have consequences, and the interactive element will provide feedback on the impact of those decisions. This approach will allow readers to understand the importance of thorough planning, stakeholder engagement, and effective project execution in government projects.

Section 3

Managing Project Scope, Time, and Resources

Managing project scope, time, and resources are critical for project success. This section will feature an interactive simulation where readers will be presented with a scenario of a government project with scope, time, and resource challenges. Readers will have to make decisions on how to address these challenges and balance competing priorities. The interactive simulation will provide immediate feedback on the consequences of each decision, helping readers understand the complexities and trade-offs involved in managing project constraints.

Section 4

Adhering to Government Reporting and Documentation Requirements

Government projects often require strict adherence to reporting and documentation requirements. In this section, we will present an interactive infographic that outlines the key reporting and documentation milestones in a government project lifecycle. Readers can click on each milestone to access detailed information about the specific requirements and best practices for meeting those requirements. The interactive element will engage readers and help them navigate the complexities of government reporting and documentation.

Section 5

Mitigating Risks and Ensuring Project Success

Risk management is essential in government projects to mitigate potential challenges and ensure project success. In this section, we will provide an interactive risk assessment tool designed to assist readers to identify and evaluate risks specific to government projects. The tool will guide readers through a series of questions and provide risk mitigation strategies based on their responses. By actively participating in risk assessment and mitigation, readers will develop a better understanding of the importance of proactive risk management in government projects.

Chapter 10

Policy Development And Implementation

Introduction

Effective policy development and implementation are crucial for government agencies to effectively tackle societal challenges and achieve their objectives. This chapter explores the key elements of policy development and implementation, including in-depth comprehension of the policy-making process, conducting rigorous policy analysis and impact assessments, actively engaging stakeholders and gathering input, designing effective policies and programs, and implementing and monitoring policy outcomes. By focusing on these aspects, government entities can ensure that their policies are well-informed, well-designed, and successfully executed to create positive impacts on society.

Section 1

Understanding the Policy-Making Process

The policy-making process is a structured approach to formulate policies that address specific issues or challenges. In this section, we will provide an in-depth overview of the policy-making process, which typically encompasses the following stages: problem identification, agenda setting, policy formulation, decision-making, policy implementation, and evaluation. We will explain each stage and its significance, elucidating the roles of different stakeholders involved in the process. An interactive flowchart will guide readers through the policy-making journey, allowing them to click on each stage to access detailed information and real-life examples thereby facilitating a deeper comprehension of the policy-making journey.

Section 2

Conducting Policy Analysis and Impact Assessments

Policy analysis and impact assessments are vital to ensure that proposed policies are well-founded and have the intended effects. This section will explore different methods of policy analysis, such as cost-benefit analysis, SWOT analysis, and risk assessment. Additionally, we will explain the importance of conducting impact assessments to evaluate potential policy outcomes and unintended consequences. To enhance reader engagement, an interactive case study will be presented, prompting readers to perform a policy analysis and impact assessment to assess the feasibility and implications of a proposed policy. This hands-on approach will enable readers to gain practical experience in evaluating policies and understanding their potential impacts..

Section 3

Engaging Stakeholders and Gathering Input

Engaging stakeholders and gathering input is crucial to ensure that policies are responsive to the needs and preferences of the public and relevant interest groups. In this section, we will discuss the importance of stakeholder engagement and various methods to involve stakeholders throughout the policy development process, such as town hall meetings, focus groups, and online surveys. To provide practical assistance, an interactive toolkit will provide readers with valuable tips and resources to facilitate effective stakeholder engagement, including sample communication plans and engagement strategies.

Section 4

Designing Effective Policies and Programs

Designing policies and programs that can achieve their intended outcomes is a critical step in the policy development process. In this section, we will explore the key elements of policy design, such as setting clear objectives, identifying target beneficiaries, defining implementation strategies, and allocating resources. An interactive scenario-based quiz will challenge readers to design a policy or program to address a specific societal issue, offering insights into the complexities and considerations involved in policy design.

Section 5

Implementing and Monitoring Policy Outcomes

Policy implementation and monitoring are essential to ensure that policies are effectively put into action and produce the desired results. In this section, we will discuss strategies for successful policy implementation, including creating an implementation plan, coordinating efforts among various government agencies, and addressing potential implementation challenges. Additionally, we will underscore the importance of continuous monitoring and evaluation to assess policy outcomes and make necessary adjustments. An interactive dashboard will be provided as a virtual tool, enabling readers to track policy implementation progress and evaluate key performance indicators.

Chapter 11

Compliance And Legal Considerations

Introduction

Ensuring compliance with legal and regulatory requirements is of utmost importance in government projects. This chapter delves into the critical aspects of compliance and legal considerations that government agencies and project managers must navigate. We will explore key areas, including understanding legal and regulatory compliance, navigating government contract terms and conditions, adhering to labour laws, ethics, and anti-corruption policies, managing intellectual property and data protection, and handling disputes and contract amendments. By addressing these key considerations, government entities can uphold transparency, accountability, and the successful execution of projects while adhering to legal and ethical standards.

Section 1

Understanding Legal and Regulatory Compliance in Government Projects

Compliance with legal and regulatory requirements is essential to ensure that government projects are executed within the bounds of the law. In this section, we will provide an overview of the various laws and regulations that apply to government projects, such as environmental regulations, procurement laws, and public sector governance guidelines. We will also explore the consequences of non-compliance and showcase real-world examples of the implications of not adhering to legal requirements.

Section 2

Navigating Government Contract Terms and Conditions

Government contracts frequently entail terms and conditions that mandate careful navigation. In this section, we will discuss the fundamental components of government contracts, including payment terms, performance guarantees, termination clauses, and dispute resolution mechanisms. To empower readers in effectively managing contractual obligations, an interactive checklist will guide readers through the process of reviewing and negotiating government contract terms, ensuring that they are well-equipped to handle contractual obligations effectively.

Section 3

Adhering to Labour Laws, Ethics, and Anti-Corruption Policies

Labour laws, ethics, and anti-corruption policies are crucial in maintaining a fair and transparent work environment in government projects. This section will comprehensively examine labor rights and protections for employees, underscore the importance of ethical conduct in government work, and outlining strategies for preventing corruption and bribery. An interactive scenario-based quiz will challenge readers to make ethical decisions in a hypothetical government project, promoting critical thinking and encouraging ethical awareness.

Section 4

Managing Intellectual Property and Data Protection

Intellectual property (IP) and data protection are vital considerations in government projects, especially when dealing with sensitive information and innovative solutions. In this section, we will discuss strategies for protecting government-owned IP, handling third-party IP rights, and ensuring data privacy and security in compliance with relevant data protection laws. An interactive infographic will be presented, outlining best practices for IP management and data protection, empowering readers to safeguard their project's valuable assets.

Section 5

Resolving Disputes and Handling Contract Amendments

Disputes and contract amendments are common occurrences in government projects. This section will thoroughly examine alternative dispute resolution mechanisms, including mediation and arbitration, as well as strategies for effectively handling contract amendments when project requirements change. An interactive case study will present a dispute scenario, allowing readers to explore different resolution options and understand the potential impacts of each decision.

Chapter 12

Innovation And Technology

Introduction

Innovation and technology play a vital role in modernizing government operations and elevating service delivery. This chapter explores the importance of embracing digital transformation, leveraging technology for streamlined processes and service delivery, implementing data security and cybersecurity best practices, exploring emerging technologies and their potential in government work, and fostering a culture of innovation and continuous improvement. By embracing innovation and leveraging technology, government organizations can amplify their effectiveness, efficiency, and responsiveness to the needs of citizens.

Section 1

Embracing Digital Transformation

Digital transformation involves integration of technology into every aspect of government operations to enhance efficiency and improve service delivery. In this section, we will discuss the benefits of digital transformation in government, such as streamlined processes, enhanced accessibility, and improved citizen engagement. We will explore successful case studies of government organizations that have embraced digital transformation and highlight key lessons learned. An interactive discussion will invite readers to share their experiences and insights on the challenges and opportunities associated with digital transformation.

Section 2

Leveraging Technology for Efficient Processes and Service Delivery

Technology provides plethora of tools and solutions that can optimize government processes and improve service delivery. This section will delve into the use of technology for automating manual tasks, streamlining workflows, and enhancing communication and collaboration. We will explore examples of technology applications in various government sectors, such as e-government services, digital document management, and online service portals. To provide an immersive experience, an interactive demonstration will be presented, allowing readers to explore a virtual government service portal and experience the benefits of technology-driven service delivery.

Section 3

Data Security and Cybersecurity Best Practices

With the increasing reliance on technology, data security and cybersecurity have become paramount in government operations. This section will discuss the importance of protecting sensitive data and ensuring secure systems and networks. We will explore best practices for data security, including encryption, access controls, regular security audits, and comprehensive employee training. Additionally, we will discuss the significance of cybersecurity awareness and implementation of incident response plans. An interactive case study will present readers with cybersecurity scenarios, challenging them to make informed decisions to mitigate risks and protect government data.

Section 4

Exploring Emerging Technologies and Their Potential in Government Work

Emerging technologies have the potential to revolutionize government operations and service delivery. This section will explore the latest technological advancements, such as artificial intelligence, blockchain, Internet of Things (IoT), and big data analytics, and discuss their potential applications in government work. Through concrete examples, we will showcase how these technologies can enhance decision-making, optimize resource allocation, and improve citizen engagement. An interactive activity will allow readers to brainstorm and propose innovative uses of emerging technologies in a government context.

Section 5

Encouraging Innovation and Fostering a Culture of Continuous Improvement

To unlock the full potential of technology and stimulate innovation, government organizations must foster a culture of continuous improvement. In this section, we will discuss strategies for promoting innovation, such as creating innovation labs, encouraging cross-functional collaboration, and supporting experimentation and prototyping. We will explore the importance of leadership support and employee engagement in driving innovation. An interactive discussion will invite readers to share their ideas for fostering innovation within their respective government organizations.

Chapter 13

Post-Acquisition Success
And Relationship Management

Introduction

Post-acquisition success and relationship management are crucial aspects of government projects. This chapter extensively covers the key considerations for delivering successful projects on time and within budget, building strong relationships with government agencies and stakeholders, managing expectations and ensuring customer satisfaction, leveraging project success for future opportunities, and maintaining long-term partnerships for repeat business. By emphasizing these areas, government entities and project managers can enhance project outcomes, foster collaboration, and pave the way for future success.

Section 1

Delivering Successful Government Projects on Time and Within Budget

Ensuring timely and budget-conscious project delivery is paramount for government project success.. In this section, we will explore strategies and best practices for effective project delivery. Interactive case studies will showcase successful government projects that were completed on schedule and within budget. Readers will have the opportunity to click on various project milestones to understand the key factors that contributed to their success. These factors may include effective project planning, efficient resource allocation, risk management, and proactive stakeholder engagement.

Section 2

Building Strong Relationships with Government Agencies and Stakeholders

Building strong relationships with government agencies and stakeholders is vital for project success and future opportunities. This section will delve into the importance of relationship management and provide practical tips for establishing and nurturing these relationships. An interactive toolkit will offer readers guidance on effective communication, collaboration, and stakeholder engagement strategies. Readers can click on different tools to access resources such as templates, sample communication plans, and stakeholder engagement frameworks.

Section 3

Managing Expectations and Ensuring Customer Satisfaction

Managing expectations and ensuring customer satisfaction are key elements of successful project management. In this section, we will discuss the importance of setting clear project expectations, effectively managing stakeholder requirements, and implementing robust project monitoring and feedback mechanisms. An interactive survey will enable readers to assess their organization's customer satisfaction practices and receive tailored recommendations for improvement. Furthermore, readers can also explore real-life examples of government projects that effectively managed expectations and achieved high levels of customer satisfaction.

Section 4

Leveraging Project Success for Future Government Opportunities

Project success can open doors to future government opportunities. In this section, we will explore strategies for leveraging project success to secure future projects. An interactive roadmap will guide readers through the process of identifying potential opportunities, showcasing project achievements, and leveraging relationships and networks. Readers will be able to click on different milestones to access resources and tips for maximizing their chances of securing future government projects.

Section 5

Maintaining Long-Term Partnerships and Repeat Business

Maintaining long-term partnerships is key to securing repeat business in the government sector. In this section, we will discuss the importance of relationship continuity, delivering value beyond project completion, and fostering a culture of trust and collaboration. To illustrate these concepts, an interactive case study will be presented, showcasing a successful long-term partnership between a government agency and a vendor, demonstrating the strategies employed to maintain a mutually beneficial relationship. Readers can click on different elements to explore the key factors that contributed to the partnership's longevity and success.

"Smooth Sailing Through Government Project" is a comprehensive guide to succeeding in the government sector. By implementing the insights and strategies provided in each chapter, you can confidently navigate the complexities of government procurement, project acquisition, and execution. Whether you are a seasoned professional or a newcomer, this book equips you with the tools to excel in the public sector and drive positive change in society.

Remember that each day presents an opportunity for growth and innovation. Embrace digital transformation, stay informed about emerging technologies, and maintain a commitment to excellence in your government endeavours.

Thank you for embarking on this enlightening journey with us. May the knowledge gained here empower you to make a lasting impact in the government sector, driving positive change and contributing to the betterment of society.

With best wishes,

Dr. Siya Seth